WATCHFUL
WOLVES

by Ruth Berman

photographs by William Muñoz

Lerner Publications Company • Minneapolis

Website address: www.lernerbooks.com

Curriculum Development Director: Nancy M. Campbell

Words in *italic type* are explained in a glossary
on page 30.

Library of Congress Cataloging-in-Publication Data

Berman, Ruth.
    Watchful wolves / by Ruth Berman ; photographs
by William Muñoz.
        p.   cm. — (Pull ahead books)
    Includes index.
    Summary: Describes the dynamics of a wolf pack,
the way in which wolves hunt, and where they live.
        ISBN 0-8225-3600-5 (lib. bdg. : alk. paper). —
        ISBN 0-8225-3606-4 (pbk. : alk. paper)
    1. Wolves—Juvenile literature. [1. Wolves.] I. Muñoz,
William, ill. II. Title. III. Series.
QL737.C22B455 1998
599.773—dc21   97-38027

Manufactured in the United States of America
1 2 3 4 5 6 – JR – 03 02 01 00 99 98

The front paw of a grown wolf makes a track about this size.

Is your hand larger, smaller, or the same size?

A wolf is howling. She is looking
for her family *pack.*

She finds them!

Wolves say hello with their bodies.
How do you use your body
to say hello?

Each wolf pack has a *territory.*

A territory is the place where
a wolf pack lives and hunts.

Wolves can smell other wolves
that come into their territory.

This mother and her pups
live in a *den.*

The den is dry and safe.
How is your house like a den?

These pups are old enough
to rest outside.

The strongest wolf is the leader
of the pack.

Look! The stronger wolf is on top.

Wolves are *carnivores.*

Carnivores eat other animals.

Wolves
need to
be good
hunters.

Do you
know how
they hunt?

They use their ears to hear
animals moving around.

They use their *sense of smell*
to help them find animals.

These wolves are running quickly
to catch an animal.

This wolf is watching and
waiting for an animal.

If an animal comes near,
the wolf will *pounce* or jump on it.

A wolf pack often hunts
and eats together.

After dinner, this wolf is ready
for a nap!

This is a red wolf.

What colors can you find in its fur?

This is a gray wolf.

What colors
can you
find here?

How does thick fur help a wolf?

When wolves get too warm,
they *pant.*

They pant
to stay cool.
How do
you stay
cool?

A wolf is a *mammal.*

Mammals are animals
with fur or hair.

Baby mammals can drink milk
from their mothers.

How many mammals
can you name?

Wolves howl and hunt.

They play and live
in a family pack.

Wolves are a lot like you and me!

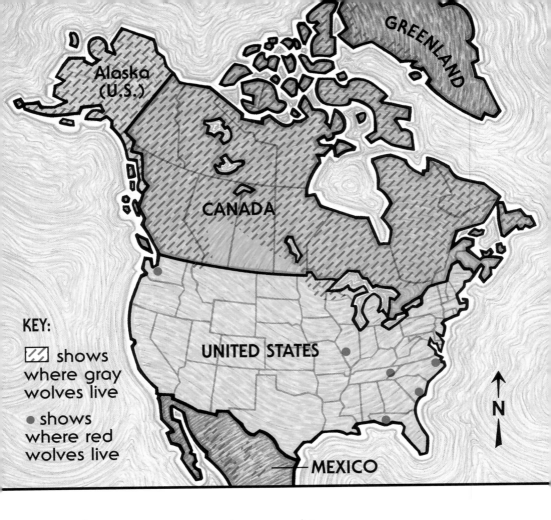

KEY:

□ shows where gray wolves live

• shows where red wolves live

Find your state or province on this map.
Do wolves live near you?

Parts of a Wolf's Body

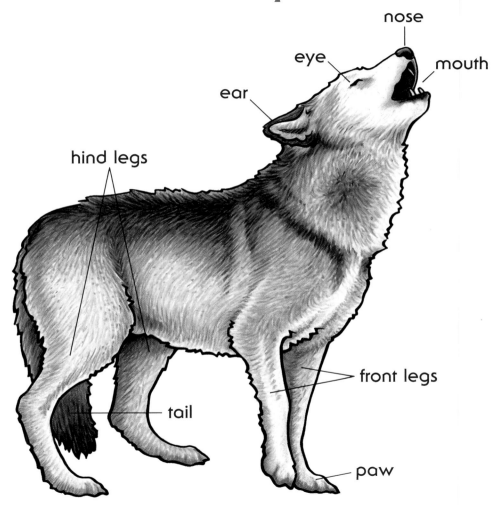

nose

eye

mouth

ear

hind legs

front legs

tail

paw

Glossary

carnivores: animals that eat other animals

den: a cozy, safe place to live

mammal: an animal that has fur or hair and drinks mother's milk when young. (Some mammals are humans, bears, wolves, bats, and whales.)

pack: a group of wolves that live as a family

pant: to breathe quickly to cool down

pounce: to jump onto something suddenly

sense of smell: one of the five ways animals get information about things around them. (The other four senses are seeing, hearing, touching, and tasting.)

territory: an area where an animal lives and hunts

Hunt and Find

- wolves **howling** on pages 4, 26
- how wolves **hunt** on pages 14–18
- wolf **packs** on pages 5, 15, 18
- **places** wolves live on pages 6, 8, 25, 28
- wolves **playing** on page 27
- wolf **pups** on pages 9, 25, 31

The publisher wishes to extend special thanks to our **series consultant,** Sharyn Fenwick. An elementary science-math specialist, Mrs. Fenwick was the recipient of the National Science Teachers Association 1991 Distinguished Teaching Award. In 1992, representing the state of Minnesota at the elementary level, she received the Presidential Award for Excellence in Math and Science Teaching.

Robin Buckley

About the Author

Ruth Berman was born in New York and grew up in Minnesota. As a child, she spent her time going to school and saving lost and hurt animals. Later, Ruth volunteered at three zoos and got her degree in English. She enjoys writing science books for children. She has written six books in Lerner's Pull Ahead series. Her other books include *Ants, Peacocks,* and *My Pet Dog* (Lerner Publications) and *Sharks* and *American Bison* (Carolrhoda Books). Ruth lives in California with her dog, Hannah, and her two cats, Nikki and Toby.

Sandy Muñoz

About the Photographer

William Muñoz has worked as a nature photographer for over 20 years. You can see his pictures of animals and plants in many books for children. Some of these books include *Ants, Apple Trees,* and *Polar Bears* (Lerner Publications) and *Horses, Dogs,* and *Cattle* (Carolrhoda Books). William lives with his wife and son in Missoula, Montana.